Satisfied

With Not Being

Satisfied

Sandra DeShawn Cavette

HATCHBACK Publishing

Genesee Michigan

Published by: HATCHBACK Publishing
              Genesee, Michigan 48437
              Since 2005

ISBN: 978-1-948708-34-0

Printed in the United States of America
10 9 8 7 6 5 4 3 2 1

For Worldwide Distribution

Satisfied

With Not Being

Satisfied

Table Of Contents

Introduction- Pleasing People or Pleasing God.....6

Eye Opener.....9

Leaving The Past.....18

Marriage Get In The Boat -Try Something New...26

Your Spouse- Your Friend.....40

Forgiveness.....49

Know Your Worth.....53

Relationships.....58

Mentor/Mentee.....71

Healthy Nuts and Seeds.....77

Knowing Your Purpose.....82

We Are The Teacher-Our Children.....85

Prayer.....89

Music and The Moment.....97

Your Heart.....104

Your Mind.....112

Reading.....120

Life Changers.....127

Words Have Power.....143

The Pastor's Wife.....149

Technology & Social Media.....162

Reminiscing/The Good Old Days 174

Talking Clay- A Conversation With God.....194

Satisfied With The Wrong Man.....201

Satisfaction Survey – Are You Satisfied?.....203

Book/Song List.....206

Author Bio.....212
Bibliography.....214

Introduction

Pleasing People or Pleasing God

So many times we allow people, obstacles and circumstances to stop us from achieving our goals. God has equipped each one of us with everything we need to fulfill our purpose. He has given us strength to fight the enemy and patience to wait for the right doors to open so we can walk into our destiny. Sometimes, we get in a hurry and miss our opportunity to be in position for the next move of God.

I had a conversation with an individual while I was waiting in line to take care of some business. This lady began to inquire about my employment. She expressed that she always wanted to work in the field of education but she ended up getting married, having children, and she never took the time to pursue her dream and passion. She stated that she had a decent job which paid well. She was influenced by her family and peers to stay where she was and be satisfied with her life.

This happens to people quite often. We know what we want, where we want to live, what we want to do, and who we want to do it with but we settle for what is easy and convenient. I admonish each and every one of you to stop allowing other people to persuade you from doing what you want to do.

Life is too short for you to waste time trying to please everyone but God. It's time to be serious and allow your dreams and goals to come to fruition.

The Inspirational Songs

Music is important in our lives. It can set the mood for your day. It may be a jingle in a commercial, a ballad or listening to your favorite artist. If you think back to the days when you were young you will probably remember songs like *Twinkle, Twinkle Little Star, Can You Show Me How To Get To Sesame Street*? or *Yes Jesus Loves Me*. Maybe you memorized to the Grammar Rock song, *Conjunction, Junction What's Your Function?* I still remember The Theme songs from *Mr. Roger's neighborhood, The Jefferson's, The Brady Bunch*, and *Good Times*.

God's power is still magnified in the hymn songs like *Blessed Assurance, Amazing Grace, Near The Cross*, and *There Is Power In The Blood.* No matter what genre of music you listen to it will become a part of you... if you listen long enough.

There is nothing like experiencing the Power of God in worship and praise. It has been said when you're feeling uplifted you listen to the music, but when you need your spirit lifted you listen to the lyrics. Your mood will be changed if you begin to sing a song, listen to a song or you allow the song to minister to you. This is why I chose to start each chapter out with various inspirational songs. May God bless you to feel His presence as you allow the music and lyrics to bring peace to your mind, soothe your soul, and comfort your heart.

Eye Opener

Inspirational Songs:

Never A Day ~United Tenors

When You Praise ~ Fred Hammond

The Mender ~ Donald Lawrence

I thought I was going to a routine exam. To my surprise, this eye exam changed my life drastically. As I began my exam, the doctor asked me to cover my eye and read the chart. I told him I could not see the letters. He increased the size. I told him I still could not see the letters on the chart. After increasing the letters to the largest size, he asked me my name. I told him my name. He said he wanted to make sure he had the correct patient. He said it had been less than two years since my last visit, and at that appointment I had 20/20 vision in both eyes. He began to ask me questions like: If I had any injuries to my eyes since my last visit? Did I notice anything different with my eyesight? Do I have headaches?

He asked what happened to my vision. He said he had never seen anything like it in his thirty plus years of practice. My eyesight had went from 20/20 vision to 20/400. I had a macular hole. He said what he was seeing was unheard of. After things calmed down, he checked my other eye. It was fine. He had to give me eye drops to dilate my eye.

As I waited for my eyes to dilate, I started covering each eye to see if I could see things at a distance.   As I tried to see with my right eye, I noticed things were very blurry and some things – I couldn't even see until I uncovered both of my eyes. As I looked over my left shoulder, I noticed a clay replica of an eye on the brown counter top. The doctor picked the replica up and explained the parts of the eye to me. He stated a macular hole is a break in the macula, which is located in the center of the retina. The macula controls the central vision which is used for the seeing, reading, driving, and to see fine details. A macular hole can cause distorted and blurred vision. As he continued to explain this hole in detail, he asked if my husband and I had any questions.

I was sitting there in a total state of shock. The room was silent. All you could hear was the clock on the wall as the second hand moved from right to left. The more the doctor spoke, the faster my heart raced. The beat increased from a lullaby being sung to an infant to the thump of a bass drum in a marching band.

I felt numb, scared, and confused all at the same time. I was quiet while my husband asked questions like: What caused it? Can anything be done to correct her vision? Is it hereditary?

I couldn't speak for a while. I was overwhelmed. All I could do was pray and ask God to help me. This was definitely not the time to lose my composure. I know God is a healer. He healed several blind people in the Bible. A man saw men as trees and God healed him and his sight was restored (see St. Mark 8:24). I just started to pray and speak life.

I thank God for my husband who was right there every step of the way. It makes all the difference to have a praying man of God in your life that will support you through your ups and downs. Every time I would feel discouraged, he always would have an encouraging word and a scripture for me. For everyone who doesn't believe in God and the power of prayer, there will come a time in your life when you will have what I call a "Jesus Reality Check."

After you check with all your sources and you see that people cannot help you, you will know that

God and God alone is the only one that can help you. God has never failed me yet. I'm so glad I learned at an early age to depend on God. I don't worry about a situation I cannot change. God is Jehovah Rapha – "the Lord who heals." I put all my trust and confidence in God and not man!

The doctor continued the exam and wrote so many notes in my chart, I started getting impatient. *If he can't do anything to help my situation, I know a God who can.* He continued to write for another twenty minutes and then he referred me to a Vitreo Retinal Specialist. We finally left the doctor's office. *What do I do now? What is my next move? Lord you already know my condition.* I tried to keep it all together. All I could do was cry on my husband's shoulder.

I went to the specialist and they scheduled me for surgery two weeks later. In those two week, I had a serious talk with God. I remembered so many sermons that were preached on healing. I tried to keep my mind on spiritual things but the enemy brought all kinds of thoughts to my mind. All the "what ifs." *What if your eye is worse after the surgery? What if instead of doing surgery on the eye with the macular hole, they operate on the wrong eye? What if the anesthesia doesn't work and you feel pain before the surgery is over? What if you are allergic to the medicine they give you and everything goes wrong?*

I had to combat all the negative thoughts with positive thoughts. I truly had to encourage myself. I prayed for wisdom and strength to go through this test. I did not want to go through surgery but that was what I needed to do for my healing.

One of my worst fears was going through another surgery and something goes wrong. Every time I felt myself getting depressed, I immediately began to pray to turn everything around. In Romans 8:28, it states, *All things work together for your good.* I didn't understand everything that was going on but I knew God was going to turn every trial into a triumph. I didn't know how He was going to do it, but I was sure He would do it. I refused to allow anyone that had doubt to change my thoughts. I only told the people I thought could pray, and touch and agree with me. Anyone who had wavering faith or doubted everything would turn out favorably, I immediately cut ties with them. The effectual prayers of the righteous availeth much. As long as I had the prayers of the righteous friends and family, I was able to maintain peace in my heart.

Leaving The Past

Inspirational Songs:

Wait On Him ~ *John P. Kee*

There Is A King In You ~ *Donald Lawrence*

Full And Complete ~ *Walter Hawkins and The Love Crusade Choir*

PAST = Problems, Attitudes, Situations and Things

Several questions come to my mind when I think about the past. What we used to do? How the past does affects us? Is your past important? Without realizing it, we carry *something* from the past with us everywhere we go. It comes out in our conversations and will show up in our attitudes.

Our past is powerful. It will live inside us and keeps us from moving forward. If you listen to people talk and take note of their conversation, you will hear something about the past.

I know the past can hold several different situations such as a difficult childhood, disappointments, separation, divorce, sickness, death, financial problems or job loss. No matter how painful our past may have been, for some reason we often choose to not let it go. In order to simplify our lives and move to the next blessing, we must choose to make a clean break and leave the past behind.

Sometimes we allow ourselves to remain in the past because we are afraid of what the present holds. Maybe you've been hurt in a previous relationship and you told yourself you would never love or trust again. If this is your mentality with every person you meet, you are probably still dealing with past hurts.

I've heard statements like, "No man or no woman can be trusted." You shouldn't allow someone from your past to stop you from a loving and fulfilling relationship. This is giving that person too much power over your destiny. There are billions of people in this world and everyone is not trying to hurt you. God will allow people to come into your life for you to minister to, mentor and help you.

Your prayers may be for help, friendship or companionship. If you know the Lord's voice, He will direct you. Everyone can't go every step with you. God's favor will have the right people you need at the right place, at the right time. If you are around a person for a while they will show their motives and intentions. Pay attention to what they say and especially what they do. Their actions will speak louder than anything they will ever say.

Remember what happened to Joseph and his brothers. They were jealous of him and his coat of many colors. Joseph's brothers sold him into slavery and then lied about what happened (see Genesis 37:12-36).

Imagine how he felt. His own brothers put him in a pit, stole his coat, and sold him like he had no worth. He was sold to the Ishmaelites for twenty pieces of silver and ended up in Egypt as a slave. They lied and told his father he was dead. In the end God turned everything around for a blessing for him. His brothers didn't realize they couldn't control his destiny. No one can stop the blessings God has prepared for you.

When we experience offenses in our life, it seems like a double whammy when it comes from family and close friends. That's the time we have to rely on God to bring us out of whatever situation we are in. Many times we put too much confidence in people. As a rule, I usually listen to what people say but I really don't put complete confidence in everything they say. Sometimes people have good intentions. They talk good but don't keep their word all the time.

God is the only one we can fully rely on and give our total confidence. I was taught to be a person of my word. So if I commit to something I try my best to do what I say I'm going to do. I'm not a no call, no show person.

I've had people tell me they were going to do things and didn't do them. So my practice is to go by what you do or show me. I refuse to allow the same people to keep disappointing me over and over again. If you are going to do something its best to just do it. If you are not, it's only common courtesy to tell a person in a reasonable amount of time that you can't fulfill your obligation. After all, now someone else have to do what you didn't do. I don't always get it right. So I thank God for never giving up on us. Life happens and there are times you will have things come up unexpectedly.

Every day we have an opportunity for God to show Himself mighty in our lives. God wants to bless us but we have to allow Him to order our steps. Philippians 3:13-14 tells us to "press towards the mark..." In order to move forward we must forget the things behind us and focus on the task that we are doing now. I'm not saying don't look back at the memories we have. I'm saying don't get stuck in the past.

We should grow stronger and better daily. Let's walk in unity and help each other accomplish our goals. Keep your mind on things that are good and peaceful. If you have thoughts that are not pleasant, immediately push them out of your mind and gravitate to things that are pleasant and good. Our thoughts will become our actions if we dwell on them long enough.

Marriage - Get In The Boat

(Try something new)

Inspirational Songs:

Lost Without You ~ *CeCe and BeBe Winans*

Wedding Song ~ *John P. Kee The New Life Community Choir*

Just For Me ~ *Karen Clark Sheard*

It is imperative to stay in touch with what is going on in your spouse's life. You can live in the same house and not be informed about what is *really* going on with them. In the fast pace world we live in, you can get busy doing things individually. If you have your own automobile and your mate has their own vehicle, you can see each other in passing and have two separate agendas. You may also have your set of friends and your mate their set of friends and rarely make plans that include your spouse.

I've met people and I never knew they were married. They don't wear a wedding ring. They are always by themselves. I have never heard them mention having a spouse. I was surprised when someone told me some of these people were married. I'm not saying that you have to be with your spouse all the time but you do need to spend some quality time together.

I'm astonished at the people that don't take the time to make their spouse a daily priority. I hear them complain about the lack of support from their mate. When they begin to converse and sometimes complain about their mate not being with them, I listen to the whole conversation before I respond. I generally ask the question, "Does your spouse know how you feel about the issue?" Their reply is usually, "No, they don't really know how I feel." Next, they respond, "I get tired of asking them to spend time with me and they act like I'm not a priority." Some spouses are just tired of the excuses that they are given as to why they don't spend time together.

I admonish couples to make it a daily practice to pray for and with their mate. I also encourage them to make an effort to discuss their feelings. After all, their mate is the one who ultimately decides whether or not they want to change their plans and spend more time with them. You don't want to compete with others for quality time with our mate. That is very unacceptable and quite detrimental to a healthy and loving relationship. If you are going to be in a marriage, you have to be together when it is necessary. And you don't want to be in a relationship where you feel empty and alone all the time.

That's why it is important to have regular date nights and stay involved in each other's lives. Some people work opposite shifts which makes it a challenge to synchronize their calendars but it can be done. It might take a little more effort. But whatever is important to you, you will do it. You don't want to give the enemy any room to step in. Once he is in the door he will take over. This is why you need to have good communication between each other at all times. You may have to be creative and try to meet for lunch and make your date night time on the weekend.

No matter what it takes, you have to be willing to do what you need to do to have a healthy marriage. You really don't have to spend a lot of money to have a date night. There are various things you can do for entertainment. Discuss what you want to do. Maybe it is watching movies, going to a game, museum, sports outing, or attend seminars. Every day is an opportunity to make your marriage stronger.

Find out what your mate would like to do and surprise them. Don't be stuck in the same old routine. Some people wear the same thing, cook the same thing, look the same way, and never surprise their mate. Change something: your clothes, lingerie, hair, perfume, furniture, your attitude and rekindle the fire you once had.

Keep the relationship fresh, exciting and renewed. Step out of the box. You may be surprised what you might like if you try something new. Be willing to give and be able to receive. It's a great big world to explore. Try to be open to doing some things that your mate likes. Intimacy is important in a marriage.

I hear about so many odd, extreme, unconventional, and unusual traditions that are going on in marriages today. I can see why the divorce rate is so high. People are allowing the opinions of others to dictate how their marriage should be. The Bible is still the standard for a blessed union. It speaks on how a husband and wife should interact (see Ephesians 5:22-33). A man should look for a wife not a wife look for her husband. Most people want something good. Proverbs 18:22 lets us know that wives are good things.

When we allow God to be the center of our marriage, our union will be blessed. People don't fully recognize or comprehend what they are saying when they say, "I do". They go into marriage thinking if this does not work I will say, "I don't". Too many couples lack marriage counseling, information, and dedication to sustain their marriages. There is lack of trust, love, time, money, preparation, respect, and communication. Take time out to pray, hug, laugh, bond, kiss, caress, excite, relax, tickle, massage, talk, read, motivate, and give your best love at all times. Stop putting limits on your marriage. Allow your passion and desires to overflow. Marriage can and will work if we stop saying no and start saying yes to being committed to becoming a better mate. Then love will abide in our hearts and you will see each other in a different light. If the romance, desire, and passion is gone, you need to do what is necessary to bring the fire back into your heart. Start today. Don't wait another minute. Love is the key. God can restore the love that was once lost. Step into the boat. What boat? The love boat!

Have you ever had a boat or ship experience? Some of us have experienced the luxury of a cruise ship, maybe you've been on a paddle boat, rode on a pontoon or kayak. No matter what the boat was, you have to have a boat/ship experience. Let me tell you about my experience.

It was not my desire to be on a boat fishing but my husband enjoys it. One day he wanted to go fishing in Canada. He couldn't find anyone to go with him. So I decided to go. I went, not really knowing how the day was going to turn out. When we arrived at our destination, I began to look around. As far as my eyes could see, I saw miles of deep blue water and black and white seagulls flying above my head. I inhaled and exhaled as to say, *Lord, what have I gotten myself into.* I immediately said a prayer. *You can do this.* My mind was saying one thing, but my body was saying something else. I started second guessing the whole thing. I began to wonder about what would, and could go wrong with us in this eighteen foot boat. Next, I put on my neon orange lifejacket. I made sure the three orange Velcro straps were tight and the long khaki laces were tied as tight as I could stand them. *Was I really ready for this adventure?*

As I stared out into the miles of water, I must have had a scared look on my face because my husband kept asking me was I okay. While he assisted me onto the boat, I took another deep breath and tried to act like I had no fear. Then I heard the gears shift, and the motor rev. My heart was beating as fast as a cheetah on the prowl for its' next meal. As the boat ride began it started out bumpy and my husband said, "Hold on to your hat." I placed my right hand on my beige, straw sun hat and used my left hand to wipe water off my face and glasses at the same time.

As the ride continued my husband asked me was I okay several more times. It seemed as if we were flying across the water. I was determined not to lose my rhinestone straw hat, keep the water off my face, and look calm and collected at the same time. I mustered up enough strength to say, "Yes, I'm okay as long as I'm with you." *If he asks me that one more time, I'm going to tell him he can turn this boat around and take me back to shore. After all I didn't sign up for all this on a Monday or any other day of the week.*

The twenty minute ride to the infamous walleye fishing hole seemed like it took forever. I said, "Thank you Jesus! We finally made it. Now I can relax and chill."

Oh, but to my surprise, my husband started asking a number of questions. "Can you pass me that? Can you hold this pole? Can you give me that lure over there? Can you put the bait on this pole?"

I replied, "How far are we from shore? Does this radio work on this boat? Why do you think I want to do anything but relax? You are asking me to do too much. I want to chill and relax like I see the people doing on the fishing shows on television."

We both had a good laugh. After we began to catch fish the day became more exciting. I learned about the different lures and types of fish. I also learned about the fish locator and gathered information about the lake we were on. I actually had fun fishing with him that day. I'm glad I didn't have him take me back to shore. I would have missed an exciting activity. I enjoyed it so much that we went back fishing several times after that.

I was glad I got in the boat and stepped out of my

comfort zone.

When I thought I was just getting in the boat for

fishing trip, God was trying to give my husband and

I fellowship, friendship, courtship, and

companionship in order to strengthen our

relationship, so we will be strong enough for any

hardships.

Your Spouse - Your Friend

Inspirational Songs:

Constantly ~ *Rev. Clay Evans & The AARC Choir*

Spiritual ~ Donald Lawrence

Healing ~ Kelly Price

When I hear people talk about getting married, one of the first things that come to mind about their mate is their physical appearance. Somewhere down the line you may hear them say they want their mate to be their friend. Nowadays, the word friend is used so loosely, it makes me wonder if some people know what a friend really is. I hear a lot of people say they have a vast number of friends. Maybe they mean they have a vast number of associates.

A friend can be defined as someone you are close to, a person who is caring and trustworthy, someone who even puts your needs ahead of theirs at times. They should have your back. This person should be able to call you out when you are not living right and doing the things that are detrimental to you. This goes both ways. They should be able to agree to disagree and not jeopardize your relationship. A best friend understands and accepts your strengths and weaknesses. This speaks volumes. You may think someone is your friend and later on you find out they were the one who was stabbing you in the back. This happens more times than we really can talk about. My parents told me if you are blessed to have two or three good friends in a lifetime, you are truly blessed. My father used to say, "A friend is a person who knows all about you and is still willing to be your friend." I didn't really understand that statement fully when I was a young child back then but I do now.

As I have talked to couples, some of them revealed that they were not friends at first. Research shows that couples who were friends first usually have better relationships in the long run. Many couples who were not friends first have a harder time lasting in long term relationships. Some couples are so infatuated with the other's character traits that they never really got to know the real person they were marrying. Other couples that rush into marriage because of pressure and hormones out of control, have a tendency to fail. Some of them don't even last one year to two years.

Your spouse doesn't have to be your best friend, but in a lot of cases they are your best friend. It is wise to have other friends (generally of the same sex) you can trust and depend on. The more you learn about a person while you are dating the better. You can see how their relationship is with God. You can learn about how they treat their family, friends, and favorites. Also, you can learn how they save and spend their money. During this time you can see how they handle anger, disappointment, rejection and what kind of work ethic they have. You will not learn everything about a person while being friends but the real person will show up. You can only hide for so long. You just need to pay attention.

Before I got married, I had an older gentlemen ask me and some friends about our boyfriends. He asked us several questions like: Did we know if our boyfriends had bad tempers? Have you seen your boyfriend mad before? How does he treat his mother and other females? Does he go to church? Is he involved in church? Does he pay tithes in his church? Is he stingy? Does he work? Is he a gentlemen? Does he have a good work ethic? Does he pay for things or do you have to pay when you all go out? Do your parents like them?

He advised us to find out as much as we could about our boyfriends before we get too serious. Some of us thought he was being noisy but it was actually good advice. These are some general things you need to know about a person if you plan on marrying them.

If you don't keep friendship in your marriage, you set yourself up for a relationship more like a business partner. I mean you are there just because you need that person to do something like watch the children, fix what's broken around the house, take care of minor repairs, do household duties and/or pay their part of the bills. This definitely is not God's plan for a thriving marriage. When people consistency place their spouses needs at the bottom of their priority list you are asking for your marriage to end up with infidelity or demise. Always keep in mind when you are not spending time with your spouse something or someone else is. I've seen people neglect their spouse and then get an attitude when someone else gives them some attention. People know when there is tension in relationships. Your whole demeanor changes when that person comes around. Generally a person knows what to do to correct the negative behavior. A good place to start is communicating. Talking about the issue will allow both individuals to express their feelings. From there you can see what direction you need to go in. So many times couples shut down, either avoid talking to each other, or only say a few words, some people just text each other. Either way once the communication stops the breakdown of the relationship will follow if you don't start to repair everything. You and your spouse can make the marriage work and remain friends if you both put forth an effort to regain your friendship and rekindle the love you once shared. Take time to get together weekly, don't leave out the intimacy. When you both put your pride aside and make each other a priority the possibilities are endless to how strong the friendship and marriage will be. It's ultimately left up to you. It's a beautiful thing for your mate to be your best friend, lover and

soulmate.

Forgiveness

Inspirational Songs:

Peace, Be Still ~ *Vanessa Bell Armstrong*

Perfect Peace *~Keith Pringle*

Total Praise ~ *Richard Smallwood*

Forgiveness may be one of the most psychological and emotional experiences you will ever encounter in life. During this process your emotions vacillate like a rollercoaster ride. Your feelings can start at hurt, sadness, anger, bitterness, revenge, hostility, resentment and retaliation. They may end satisfied, thankful, happy, optimist and sometimes uncertain. Depending on whether you are asked to forgive someone, seeking forgiveness or simply trying to forgive yourself forgiveness is necessary. I recall an incident when a co-worker and I collaborated on a project. This person and I had equal responsibility for getting our work completed. Needless to say, they came late, kept making excuses why they couldn't do their part and then lied to our supervisor and said they did the majority of the work. Afterwards, they had the nerve to ask me not to tell the truth about what happened. I was angry, upset and ready to take matters in my hand. I really had to pray hard. I felt myself getting madder by the minute. My blood pressure was rising and I didn't want to have a negative attitude or cause further confusion. After I prayed about the situation, my supervisor and I talked later that day. God had already worked the situation out.

My supervisor told me that they already knew I did the majority of the work. Someone else had already told them that the other person was lying about the whole situation. The co-worker that lied conscience must have got the best of them because they came to me and asked for forgiveness. I thank God for giving me the ability to forgive this coworker and not hold a grudge. Holding on to anger can lead to hate, and a desire for revenge and retaliation. Sometimes it seems to be a lot easier to hold on to the anger and hurt feelings than to let go of them. It is best not to fall into this mindset.

These feeling are not good for your health and when you are blessed to forgive don't allow someone to keep bringing up what is buried. Negativity plus negativity will never equal a positive outcome. It is a good practice to let forgiveness be a part of your daily life. Try to overlook minor differences and look at the positive. Give people the benefit of the doubt. You can live in peace and harmony. Make the necessary changes you need to live stress free. Tell yourself drama will not take the place of peace and serenity. Say it and mean it.

Know Your Worth

Inspirational Songs:

I Can't Forget ~ *Denitra Champ*

Worth ~ *Anthony Brown and Group therAPy*

Thank You ~ *Walter Hawkins And The Love Center Choir*

In our lives when we will feel discouraged, alone, stressed and even filled with doubt about on how God sees us. Satan likes to attack our mind making us think that we have no self-worth and that God does not value us. At other times as Christians, we need reminders of how God sees us with tremendous value. We are fearfully and wondrously made (see Psalms 139:14).

Your Heavenly Father loves you. It doesn't depend on your physical appearance, where you live, your possessions, or the money in your bank account. God loves you unconditionally. You are an heir to the kingdom of God. You are royalty.

The world has stipulations on what is and is not of value. People will not always recognize your worth. Instead of trying to follow what the world wants you to be, follow the ways of the Lord. God's ways will never change. God loves you so much He gave Himself for you. If someone feels they can disrespect, belittle you, mistreat you, have you think that no one loves you, and treat you as if you don't matter, they have it all confused. God is love and He loves you. He created you in HIs image for His divine purpose.

We as the people of God are not without worth. By ourselves, we are little more than dust. Our value is inseparably connected to God's work in our lives. It is God who gives us our worth, and God to whom we have worth! We are all sinners saved by God's grace. Praise God for reconciling us back to Him. It is God's grace that has given us what we do not deserve. God gave us grace that through our transformed lives, we would understand the great treasure of His love and mercy. God sending His Son is not a demonstration of our worth, but the greatest demonstration of His love, kindness, grace, and mercy.

We were unworthy sinners, and He made us His children. Romans 3:23 says, *For all have sinned and fallen short of the glory of God.* Our value is based upon the gifts with which He has equipped us to live for Him and the position that we have in Christ. Thank you Lord for giving us worth! No man can put a value on our worth! God calls everything he created good, and we are part of His creation. God calls His creation good because of who He is, and not because of how righteous we are. There is no one righteous, not even one: (see Romans 3:10). We have been purchased by the precious blood of God's own Son. God even knows how many hairs are on your head! He knows every detail of our lives. But if you want your life to have the greatest value, then allow God to work through

you and with you.

Relationships

Inspirational Songs:

Show Me The Way ~New Jerusalem Baptist Mass Choir

We'll Understand It Better~ Kenneth Martin and The Voices In Praise

Heaven~ Bishop Neal Roberson and The Macedonia Mass Choir

We have different relationships with people. Some people we admire, tolerate, avoid, and some we despise. Several questions come to mind. How can I like this person but despise someone else? What is it about that person that changes your mood when they call or come around you?

Let's start with the man in the mirror. Ask yourself, what is it that you want out of the relationships you currently have? If you don't know what you want, you cannot expect others to know. When you are in a relationship there should be clear expectations. One of the first things you should consider is the person you are involved with someone you respect. We treat people that we respect differently than people who we are not close to.

The experiences we have in our lives dictate how we respond to others. Unfortunately, some people refuse to leave bitter experiences in the past, and allow them to damage future relationships. This is not conducive for a healthy relationship.

We all go through problems and issues in our relationships. If someone carries these problems from their past it needs to be resolved. If you are honest with yourself, you know what your flaws are. Instead of denying and blaming others, it is imperative that you take the initiative to deal with your personal issues. When you stop making excuses for the behavior that can be corrected, you will force yourself to grow to enhance your next relationships. Take time to pray, meditate and change the negative actions.

One suggestion for improvement will be to write down the things that are good and the things that you can improve. Next, make a conscience decision to work on the adverse behavior and embrace the positive. Sometimes we are our worst critics.

Most people want and need good relationships. Developing this is going to take time, energy and social skills. Building close relationships with co-workers, family members and friends can be achieved. Sometimes it's a matter of willingness to take time to build and sometimes repair previous relations. Every relationship is unique and is developed for many reasons. One basic principle is to keep them exciting, rewarding, and meaningful through trials, transitions, and the triumphs life brings.

Communication is one key element in any relationship. Honesty is essential to begin this process. When both people feel comfortable expressing their desires, needs, dreams, and fears trust will be strengthened. Non-verbal clues like eye contact, nodding your head, facial expressions, leaning forward, and a touch on the arm, shows you are engaged.

Studies have shown the importance of touch. An affectionate touch boosts the level of oxytocin, a hormone that influences attachment and bonding in the body. A touch is a part of a healthy relationship. Unwanted or inappropriate touching can cause people to withdraw. Know the parameters of each relationship. Life would be lonely without physical contact with others. When there is a breakdown of communication, people stop relating well, if stress is added to this equation this can lead to disconnect. You can work through whatever problem you are facing if you are communicating.

Don't assume other people know what you want. People are not mind readers. It is much easier to be clear about what your needs are to avoid any confusion. People who don't freely express their needs can harbor anger, resentment, and misunderstanding. When you practice expressing your needs you are able to keep the lines of communication clear. Mean what you say and say what you mean.

Communication can make or break any relationship. It is very difficult to hear what the other person is saying if you both speak at the same time. You may need to slow down, stop talking, and really focus on what the other person is saying. Next, you may need to repeat what they said to make sure you heard what they were trying to convey to you. Some issues need to be discussed face to face and not written. Avoid talking about important issues by email, letters, and text messages. This process can be misinterpreted. Choose the way you word things. Some words may come across harsh. Provide feedback to the other person. Find the right time and place to talk. Some discussions are not appropriate for the general public. Locate a place where you can both talk freely and comfortably.

Be aware of and try to control your emotions. When you are stressed, you are more likely to send confusing signals and misread others. How many times have you done or said something you later regretted? It is better to wait until you are calm and relaxed to give an appropriate response. Give yourself time to think rationally. Don't rush your response. Pause for a few minutes and collect your thoughts. Maintain an even tone and speak directly, and clearly. When things get heated, bring down the emotional intensity by taking a deep breath and speaking slowly. If you have to be silent, stop speaking for a few moments and then continue speaking. This allows you to regain your thoughts and give your conclusion to the matter.

No two people are the same. You will not always agree on everything all the time. Agreements and disagreements are common. Learn to compromise. It can strengthen your relationship or destroy it. Failure to compromise can threaten your relationships. No one can make you happy one hundred percent of the time. Be realistic and find the best way for you and others to relate. You may have to meet in the middle or give more than you receive at times. Make compromises that create positive results without sacrificing yourself in the process. The goal is to find a healthy balance. Look at compromise as a solution not the problem. When you give you will receive.

Conflict will exist in every relationship. When communication is impossible or difficult, conflict can go unresolved. Surveys found that men and women have different communication styles. Seventy percent of men cited complaining and nagging were considered one of the top problems. Women's top complaint was the lack of validation and concern for their opinions and feelings.

Some people prefer to vent and not receive any advice. Unsolicited advice can prevent some people from opening up to you. You may be trying to help but instead it can be perceived as criticism. When in a conversation be supportive, provide encouragement and let the other person know you are there if needed. People will usually ask for help when they are looking for it. A lot of people consider themselves to be skilled communicators because they talk nonstop. Speaking is only part of the equation. Communication requires talking and listening, and most people find it easier to talk than to actively listen. The greatest communicators are known to be first and foremost great listeners.

Denial is a barrier that will cause a breakdown in communication. When a person is in denial they cannot hear, or see what others are trying to tell them. When you refuse to admit the issues, there is no change. Without admittance there will be no acceptance. Without acceptance, no change will take place.

This particular day I was trying to contact an individual. They never responded. After several failed attempts I ran into them in a local business. We greeted each other and had the following conversation:

I asked, "Did you know I was trying to contact you?"

The person said, "Yes, I know what you were calling about."

I said, "Really? You knew what I was calling you for?"

"Yes, I know you want the money back that I borrowed."

"No that's not what I wanted. I was calling you because I knew you said your money was short this month and I had extra groceries to give you. I completely forgot about the money you owed me," I relied.

Needless to say, they missed that blessing because they thought they knew what I wanted. It is never good to assume.

Mentor/Mentee

Inspirational Songs:

Jesus Will ~ Anita Wilson

God Is Great ~Ricky Dillard and New G

Gods Got A Blessing ~ Norman Hutchins

A mentor is an individual, usually older, always more experienced, who helps guide another individual's development. The mentor's role is to give advice, to guide, and support the mentee. A mentor can help the mentee improve their skills and abilities through assessment, observation, modeling, and guidance. Before any mentoring can take place a relationship must be established. Trust is crucial in this process. Sessions usually begin with exercises to get to know each other. The mentor will learn about the mentees experience, educational background, and also share his or her own background experiences. Then the mentor can build upon the mentee's strength, goals, and needs throughout this process.

Next, responsibilities and roles must be defined. The mentee typically is actively participating in lessons and receiving feedback from the mentor. Short and long term goals are established. Mentors and mentees work together to mutually agree upon the goals they are to achieve. These specific goals become the basis for the mentoring activities that will take place. Mentors provide constructive feedback to the mentee as they complete their goals. A collaboration takes place to allow the mentees the opportunity to identify concerns and solutions. Mentors encourage the mentees to be creative with their implementation for change. Once a plan is made, the mentor and mentee implement the plan and the process usually begins.

Some of the benefits of mentoring are the mentees are able to experiment with creative solutions to problems. They are able to grow and learn under the mentor's guidance. The mentee has support during transition and change. It helps to enhance and clarify career direction and advancement. The mentee is able to set attainable goals and move toward them. Networking opportunities are enhanced and the mentee is transformed into a more effective individual.

It is important to have a mentor in your life. The mentee has to want to be mentored, be dedicated and vested. You must be willing to stay long enough for growth to take place. You must be prepared to do hard work to gain the wisdom for advancement. Mentoring is more than coaching and counseling.

A spiritual mentor will pray for you and with you. They will lead you to discover your identity and purpose. Your mentor should be a role model whose life reflects Godly principles. Not only should they encourage you, they will provide you with accountability. Together you should be able to network and impact your job, church, community, and the people you encounter. You will not always agree with your mentor but the two of you should be able to discuss your view point. The mentor-mentee relationship is priceless. If you don't have a mentor I suggest you experience this relationship.

My mentor gave me a project to work on. I knew I had plenty of time to get this project done. In the interim all kinds of obstacles came up. I had some things I needed to type and my lap top crashed. My printer broke. The internet kept going out when I tried to do my research. I had to get it repaired and it took longer than the two days the repair shop said it would be. So I let my mentor know what was going on.

She said, "I understand, but I still need your project done on time."

At first I thought she was being a little unreasonable but then I remembered other people were doing other parts of this group assignment. So my part was essential in the work getting accomplished. I had to find another means to get my portion done. I needed to download Word on my tablet and was able to get the work done on time. If she wouldn't have pushed me, I probably would have procrastinated and not finished my part of the assignment. It's easy to give up. But the blessing comes when you press through all the obstacles and complete the task that need to be done.

Healthy Nuts And Seeds

Inspirational Songs:

No Defeat ~ *Hezekiah Walker*

I'm Good ~ *Tim Bowman Jr.*

Overflow ~ *Pastor William Murphy III*

When I was younger it was very common to see the adults eating nuts. I would go in the kitchen and before I got there I could smell the aroma of nuts roasting in the oven. I still remember walking to the corner store to purchase pumpkin and sun flower seeds. These are some of the benefits of nuts and seeds. I know a lot of people like chocolate but this maybe a substitute for the calories. Always check with your doctor before you change your eating habits. Remember the saying, "You are what you eat." Your body is the

temple. We only have one so let's take better care

of ourselves.

Nuts	Contains	Plus/Benefits
Almonds	Calcium, magnesium, vitamin E	Can lower cholesterol help prevent cancer selenium and lots of fiber
Brazil Nuts	protein, copper, niacin, magnesium, fiber, vitamin E,	selenium
Cedar/Pine nuts	Vitamins A, B, D, E,	contain 70% of your body's required amino acids
Cashews	copper, magnesium, zinc, iron and biotin	Good for your heart
Pecans	Vitamins E and A, folic acid, calcium, magnesium, copper, phosphorus, potassium, manganese, B	Helps lower cholesterol

	vitamins, and zinc	
Walnuts	copper, manganese, and biotin.	Good for heart and brain May help prevent chemically-induced liver damage

Seeds	Contains	Plus/Benefits
Chia seeds	omega-3 oils, protein, anti-oxidants, calcium, and fiber.	excellent source of calcium for people who don't eat dairy
Hemp seeds	omega 3 and 6 fatty acids.	cancer and heart disease prevention properties
Sunflower seeds	folate, Vitamin E, selenium and copper.	help prevent heart disease and cancer
Pumpkin Seeds	Antioxidants, zinc (carotenoids), omega-3 fatty acids	great for your immune system

Sesame Seeds	calcium, magnesium, zinc, fiber, iron, B1 and phosphorus.	They can lower blood pressure, and protect against liver damage.

Knowing Your Purpose

Inspirational Songs:

My Name Is Victory ~ *Jonathan Nelson*

Go Get It ~ *Mary, Mary*

Work Out For My Good (Live) ~*Dorinda Clark- Cole*

    God's greatest desire is for everyone to have a relationship with Him through Jesus. After you repent of your sins and accept Christ in your life, you are a vessel ready for God to use. When we turn from our own ideas and commit our lives to the mission of Christ, we will experience a closer walk with Him. This process takes having faith and belief that God has us where we are for a reason. As we walk by faith (see 2 Corinthians 5:7) and follow His directions, we will start to see the many ways God will be active, engaged, and present in our lives.

Many times when we are seeking God's will, we want to know every step before it happens. We all know God doesn't work like that. God's ways are not like our ways (see Isaiah 55:8). When we try to figure out things and make them come together they usually end torn up and incomplete. God must be number one. He is a jealous God and He will not take second place. It's God's will, God's way and God's purpose. When it comes to God's will, it is not just about a calling on our lives but it's about fulfilling the purpose and plan for our lives.

When you allow God to take complete control, not only will the Lord show you which direction you are to move, He will also reveal the appropriate time and method to take. If you are struggling with knowing God's will, pray and do what you *think* He is calling you to do. If it isn't what He desires, He'll open another door and move you to the place and position He has in mind. God wants us to rely solely on Him, and to trust Him fully. This is why He calls believers to positions that will stretch, transform, and mature them. During this process, you may not feel comfortable but God will always be there with you. Discovering your purpose will also bring you great joy, peace and change your life as you walk into your destiny.

We Are The Teacher - Our Children

Inspirational Songs:

Bring Back the Days of Yea and Nay ~ *The Winans*

Good and Bad ~ *J. Moss*

Coming Back Home ~ *BeBe Winans Featuring Brian McKnight and Joe*

Our society has sex in the forefront of everything you see on a daily basis. There was a time when people respected their bodies. Now people show everything to everyone. It's left to us to teach the young people about respecting themselves and others.

The generation I grew up in was taught to respect our elders. The majority of this generation now feels you have to earn respect. Consequently, they don't respect themselves or anyone else around them. There was a time that you could get into a fight and make up and still be friends. Now people get mad at a member of the family and want to kill the whole bloodline. It's time for us to take a stand on the Word of God and go back to what the Bible says about training up a child in way that he should go (see Proverbs 22:6). Part of the problem is if the parents don't know the right way to train the children, they can't teach them. We have to take the time to teach our children while they are young. If we want them to be Godly examples for the next generation it is our responsibility to lead and direct them by example.

Most children aren't going to just say they want to go to church. As parents, grandparents, god-parents, aunts, uncles, cousins, we may be the only spiritual role model that some children will have. We cannot afford to say it's not our responsibility to help in our homes, communities, jobs, and churches. Some people just don't know any better. Other people know and don't care. There are some that won't get involved unless something detrimental happens in their family. We are living in the last days and we don't have time to waste. God is on His way for a church without spot or wrinkle. There is always room for people who can help the Body of Christ. The enemy is cunning and he will come in through whatever way he can make

his entrance. It's time to be part of the solution.

Prayer

Inspirational Songs:

The Prayer ~ *Donnie McClurkin and Yolanda Adams*

Standing In The Need ~ *John P. Kee and the New Life Community Choir*

Pray ~ CeCe Winans

Prayer is essential to growing spiritual and knowing God. James 5:16 states...*the prayers of the righteous availeth much*. The power of prayer should never be underestimated. Prayer changes people and predicaments. When you pray it is imperative that you believe God has the power to change your circumstances. God is the omnipotent One who hears our prayers and answers them. Prayer connects us with the Almighty God, and we should expect mighty results.

One reason believers should pray is because God has commanded us to pray. In order to be obedient to His will, prayer must be part of our life.

Be careful for nothing; but in everything by prayer and supplication with thanksgiving let your requests be made known unto God (see Philippians 4:6).

Prayer allows us to offer confessions of our sins, which leads to our genuine repentance. Prayer grants us the opportunity to present our requests to our Father. He cares for us, and wants to commune with us through prayer. If we humble ourselves and pray and seek God, He will forgive our sin and will heal their land (see 2 Chronicles 7:14).

Prayer is not just asking for God's blessings. It is about intimate communication with the living God. Without communication, our spiritual relationships will fall apart. God has established prayer as part of His plan for accomplishing His will in our lives and also in the world. We are in spiritual warfare and our prayers gives us power over the enemy.

Watch and pray, that ye enter not in temptation:

The spirit indeed is willing, but the flesh is weak.

(Matthew 26:41)

Prayer is always available to us. It also keeps us from pride and it reminds us that God is sovereign and in control.

There have been times in my life when it seems like nothing was going right. Money was short and bills were due. I received multiple calls from people wanting me to help them with their issues. No matter where I turned it seems like I was the target and the punching bag for their problems. When I asked for help from the people I always helped, they had an excuse why they couldn't help me. I began to pray and ask God for help. As I completed my prayer, it seems like instantaneously God stepped in. All the pieces that were falling apart began to come together. Someone came by and gave me more money than I needed. They said they just wanted to bless me financially. Next, another person brought some extra groceries over. I made a few calls and the bill situation was worked out. Within an hour everything was back in order. The pieces that were falling apart began to come together at once. All I could do was thank God for stepping in right on time. God has never let me down. I could not have made it this far without having prayer as an essential part of my daily life. I encourage everyone to develop a prayer life.

No matter how big or small your situation may be. God cares and He wants you to live a blessed and prosperous life. Don't give up because you don't understand why every time you make one step forward, it seems like you are getting knocked three steps back. God is always there, even when you feel troubled, confused and stressed out. Your prayer can be as simple as Lord help me. No matter how many syllables or words you use to develop your prayer, God is always there to help you through. If you pray before you start your day, before you make decisions, pray during your day, and lastly before you end your day, I guarantee you things will have to change. God will either change you or He will change your situation. One way or another a change is going to happen. Prayer has always been the key to open the door of blessings. Pray and praise your way through your situation.

Don't wait until your prayer is answered to praise Him. Praise Him in advance for your breakthrough.

~ My Prayer ~

Father God, I thank You for Your grace and mercy. I ask You to forgive me for anything I said and did that was not pleasing to You. I thank You for watching over me and my family. I ask that You use me as a vessel for Your kingdom.

May the words I speak help heal and not harm. Help me to show love to each and everyone I meet. Let Your light shine through me as I go throughout this day. Order my steps, keep my mind renewed, and my soul sincere for You.

Thank You in advance for Your favor, Your protection and peace. In the mighty and matchless Name of Jesus I pray. Thank you and Amen!

Music And The Moment

Inspirational Songs:

Everything You Touch Is A Song ~ *The Winans*

Every Praise ~ *Hezekiah Walker*

I Will Bless The Lord ~ *Lord Bryon Cage*

Music is a pervasive part of our culture today. Music is important to me. I have a song in my mind and on my heart from the time I wake up until I go to bed. Just like David, I love to worship the Lord. Even when I go out throughout the day, I'm usually singing or humming a song.

Music is powerful and has a definite impact in most, if not all aspects of our lives. We hear it on telephones while we wait for our party to answer, in offices, in stores, in our vehicles, in restaurants, on elevators, in hotel lobbies, and in just about every area of our life. It permeates the airwaves and is so constant we often do not realize it is there. It is used in the media on television, in commercials, in musical programs and soundtracks. Music is used to enhance the chain of events shown on the big screen. Many radio stations offer an extensive genre of music around the clock. The accessibility of recordings allows us to program the specific music we like to listen to. With the technology we have today we can hear music at any location. Most large cities offer a plethora of music to choose from. We have choices of Gospel, Christian, Jazz, Country, Rhythm and

Blues, Rap, and the list goes on. Today's population spends innumerable hours absorbing music, whether Christian or secular.

Lyrically, music can be used as a medium for criticism, praise, questioning, reflection, and any number of other thoughts or emotions. Music can unlock a door into your soul and take your mind to another place. It can motivate you positively or negatively. The lyrical content is what makes the difference in the music.

The devil was created as the archangel Lucifer, a perfect being in every way. Lucifer was given the ability to play beautiful music. Satan eventually became a perverted being and is now the "prince of the power of the air" (see Ephesians 2:2). He does not want us to use music the way that it is intended. God deserves all glory, honor, and praise. It is satan's job to distract and manipulate us by any means necessary. When the singers and musicians praised God in song (see 2 Chronicles 5:12-13), there were over 120 priests playing trumpet alone. The musicians all played as one, to make one sound. This means the musicians played their instruments, together in harmony, and on one accord. As we worship God in music, it is important to be in unity and reverence God for who He is. Music is used to enter the presence of the Lord and to lift your spirits.

Let the word of Christ dwell in you richly... in psalms and hymns and spiritual songs, singing with grace in your hearts to the Lord.

(Colossians 3:16).

If you want your frame of mind to change, music can be a way to change your mood and feelings. Psalms 150 lets us know that God wants everything that has breath to praise the Him.

Music certainly had a major impact on King Saul as it soothed him when he was tormented by the evil spirit. David played his harp and it changed the mood of King Saul (see 1 Samuel 16:23). Music can help us to become encouraged, joyful, and ready for praise.

Music has been known to have healing properties. It is also used in professional settings for therapy. The healthcare profession uses it to enhance memory, improve communication, alleviate pain, manage stress, and promote wellness.

Music is also used to increase finances in business. There is a direct correlation to music and companies. When a survey was taken about music these were some of the results:

- 74% of people said they enjoy going to work more when music is being played, and a third are less likely to take off for sick time.
- Customers who like to hear music in stores, more than half said they spend more time in a shop that plays music.

- Customers who like to hear music in venues, a third of the customers are willing to pay 5% more in businesses that played music.

- People would rather live without sports, movies and newspapers than live without music.

- Playing the right music in your business makes consumers stay longer.

The next time we listen to music. Think about how it is used to influence us. It is used to set the atmosphere for whatever our hearts' desire, and affect our mentality. Therefore, we should use music as more than a means of entertainment.

Your Heart

Inspirational Songs:

Create In Me ~ Lawrence K. Matthews

When Sunday Comes ~ Donald Lawrence & The Tri City Singers Featuring Darryl Coley

Your Will ~ Darius Brooks

In our fast paced world we are accustomed to high levels of luxury, comforts, pleasures, and security. People believe happiness comes in material possessions, accomplishments, recognition, and the like. As a result, people develop their own agendas to climb the ladder in pursuit of happiness or success. This is the path the world follows to achieve their goals. There are people who feel if you are not at a certain level of education, drive a certain car, or live in a prestigious area, you are not successful. This is not God's design for success. The Lord does not look at our material possessions because nothing can take the place of God's favor. Man looks at the outward appearance but the Lord looks at the heart (see 1 Samuel 16:7).

God created you and can see things about you that no one else sees. He sees the deep things, the things that are hidden. He knows those inner thoughts and desires that your family and friends have no clue about. We have a tendency to assume that a person's actions are how they really feel. Most of us have experienced a person telling us one thing and actions showing us something different. But God is looking at more than just your behavior. He is looking at why you behave the way you do. He wants to know if your motives are pure, and if you are going in the direction of righteousness and godliness as compared to chasing after things which are outside of His will for your life. He's concerned about our intentions as well as our desires. Our motives and intentions are what we want to do and don't want to do. Desires on the other hand are what we are feeling or drawn to do. There is a difference.

As Christians we want to live for Christ because of everything He has done for us. He gave His life, His love, His blood, and the free gift of salvation.

Why wouldn't we want to give Him our whole heart, mind, and soul? Why wouldn't we want to do the right thing in each and every situation? This is where sin comes in the mix. Sin is more than just what we do. It is part of our being. The Bible calls it our sinful nature.

Your sinful nature is not the same thing as your heart. Your sinful nature is capable of producing evil desires, but your free will as a believer in Jesus, you decide which desires to dwell on and which ones to resist. The more we embrace good desires and righteous choices with our heart and mind, the more those bad desires will decrease in frequency and intensity.

One problem with sin is that it has the power to corrupt our motives. When this happens, we can actually start to become double-minded. This occurs when some of our intentions remain pure, while some of our motives within us become impure. Bad desires lead to bad motives and when our will acts on an evil desire rather than resisting it by God's grace, the bad motives will always increase the bad desires. God is the only one that can decrease them. God can replace them and forgive them. He does that through forgiveness by the blood of His Son.

It is amazing that God loved us enough to reach down and offer us a new heart, a new mind, and new motives. This is exactly what He does. He not only washes away every sin of those who come to the Father through the Son, but He also fills our soul with His living water. That inspirational experience leads to a new life. Through this transformation every bad motive gets replaced with good motives.

God works through the Holy Spirit. Many times we may sense a prompting from the Spirit, and we will ignore that prompting. As a result we miss God and the opportunity He has provided us. God may tell you to call someone or speak to someone but you don't do it. Don't feel bad, we all have done this. More often than not, this can happen because of fear. The fear can be of how someone will respond, fear of the unknown, and fear of rejection. These are tools of Satan.

For God has not given us a spirit of fear; but of power, and of love, and of a sound mind.

(II Timothy 1:7)

Sometimes we must remind ourselves of this fact in order to overcome all fears. Fear will paralyze us, causing us to be disobedient to the Spirit. The more we override the Holy Spirit speaking to us, the harder it becomes for us to hear God. The heart that God has given us is flesh, but it can become calloused like the rest of the world. The callous heart makes it harder for the Word to penetrate and eventually we will not even hear the Holy Spirit as He speaks.

What differentiates us from the world is the fact that we, as Christians, have a softened heart, but we have to work at keeping it pliable. When we feel promptings from God, or if we hear Him speak to us, we need to be obedient immediately. The sooner we are obedient, the easier it becomes. Before you know it, you will hear God speaking to you more. You will see Him present more opportunities for you in ministry every day. Our hearts desire should be a vessel for God to use. Thank you Lord for creating a clean heart within us! (See Psalms 51:10).

Your Mind

Inspirational Songs:

Still Here ~ The Williams Brothers

Ain't No Need To Worry ~ Ruben Studdard

It's All God ~ Soul Seekers featuring Marvin Winans

I've experienced great joy in things coming to past because of my thinking. When I have positive thoughts about how my day is going to go it usually goes good. On the other hand, I've had days in my life I would never want to repeat.

There was a day when I was worried about how some situations were going to turn out. The night before I couldn't sleep and I woke up feeling very stressful. I even said I don't think this situation is going to work out. And guess what, it didn't turn out the way I wanted or needed. I learned a lot from those days when I allowed the negative thoughts to control my actions. I learned if I was going to pray about it, I didn't have to worry about it. Our mind is powerful and controlling. We cannot afford to let anything disrupt our positive mindset.

A lot of believers are depressed and stressed simply because they allow negative thoughts to fester in their minds. We can have victory by simply changing the way we think, and controlling our thoughts. That is why the enemy always tries to get in our mind and thoughts. He doesn't want us to know the truth and the power that is in God's Word. He tries to get us to worry about things that we have no control over.

Perhaps one of the biggest differences between a victorious believer and a believer that is depressed is the thoughts that are in their minds from day to day. Yes, demonic spirits can and do play a big role in depression, fear, and the like but many times all we have to do is get our thoughts corrected. Satan will always bring thoughts to your mind and try to make you feel like no one cares, you are not forgiven and free from sin. He will also lie and try to make you doubt the truth, and make you fearful and depressed.

Finally, brethren, whatsoever things are true, whatsoever things are honest, whatsoever things are just, whatsoever things are pure, whatsoever things are lovely, whatsoever things are of good report; if there be any virtue, and if there be any praise, think on these things.

(Philippians 4:8)

We must keep our minds on good and positive things that will uplift and build us up.

Thou wilt keep him in perfect peace, whose mind is stayed on thee: because he trusteth in thee.

(Isaiah 26:3)

A change will take place when we start looking at forgiveness, blessings, and healings, instead of looking at the problems like sin, poverty, sickness, and doubt.

Take a minute to take inventory of the thoughts you've been thinking over the past few days. What kinds of thoughts were they? Are they mostly negative problems? Have they mostly been thoughts that are not in your best interest? Were they positive thoughts that build you up? How much time have you spent over the past week thinking about the goodness of the Lord and how He is your healer, deliverer, and provider? Or were they mostly thoughts concerning finances, bills and other problems?

I encourage you to stop looking at the problems in your life and begin looking at the solutions that God has provided for you. Get your mind off of all the problems, and onto the solution! If it's a healing you need, begin to search the scriptures to learn what God's Word has to say about healing for you. When my blood pressure seemed like it wouldn't stay regulated. I kept confessing healing scriptures daily. I confessed, *"You were wounded for my transgression by your stripes I'm healed,"* which is in Isaiah 53:5. If it's finances you need, then begin to research the Word and see what it has to say about your finances and God's provision. You must get your mind off all your problems, and seek God's Word for everything that you need. Matthew 7:7 says, *Ask, and it shall be given you; seek, and ye shall find*. Notice Jesus didn't say sit there and think about the problem. He said, "Seek, and you will find!"

The Bible tells us to have the mind of Christ. *Philippians 2:5 says, Let this mind be in you, which was also in Christ Jesus*. This is important. God created our minds as a combination of conscious and unconscious thoughts. These thoughts direct our mental and physical behavior. Our thoughts influence every action we take. So if we want to act like Christ, we must also think like Christ. Our minds exercise the power of reason, conceive ideas, and use judgment. It stores our intellect and distinguishes from emotion or will.

The world's approach to living is if it feels good do it. But the approach of a Christian who has the mind of Christ is I know what I think and how I feel but I'm going to do what God says to do. It's about aligning our thoughts with His thoughts before we react. Then when we react we have godly actions. This is where we can see growth. God's will is being manifested in our daily walk with Him. Once our mind is renewed, our thoughts will be changed, we will hide His words in our hearts, and have an intimate relationship with Him!

Reading

Inspirational Songs:

Being With You ~ Marcus Cole

I Adore Thee ~ John P. Kee

Hear My Voice ~ Rance Allen Group

We've all heard people say they don't have time to read. But we make time for whatever is important to us. It's really about making time, not having time. We make time for social media, appointments, and everything else.

I purchased a piece of furniture and this item came with instructions. This individual just started looking at the pictures on the box and began putting things together. They thought they knew how to put the item together correctly. After working on the furniture for over an hour, screws were left and the item was not fixed right. We had to take everything apart and start over again because this person refused to read the directions. I know I'm not the only one who has dealt with people who refuse to read and follow simple directions.

Reading is a great way to keep our brains stimulated. Studies have shown a way to possibly even prevent or slow the progress of Alzheimer's and Dementia is keeping the brain engaged and active. Playing games like chess and doing puzzles have been helpful with cognitive stimulation. Everything you read gives new information and you never know when you might need to know these facts. The more knowledge you have, the better-equipped you are for the daily challenges of life. You might lose your money, your job, your possessions or even your health but your knowledge can never be taken from you.

Reading will help with your vocabulary expansion. Being articulate and well-spoken is a great help in any profession. Knowing that you can speak to people on a higher status can also add a boost to your self-esteem. It could even assist in your career. Those who are well-read and well-spoken tend to get promotions more often than those with smaller vocabularies and lack of awareness of current events, literature, and scientific breakthroughs.

If you look at the successful people around you, one thing you will notice is they are all avid readers. This isn't the only thing that separates the successful people from average people. We all generally know some people who are avid readers and they can give you great insight in areas if you are open to listening.

Reading Christian books can also add depth to your spiritual life. This great habit will set you apart from many other people. When you are in need of a deeper depth of spiritual knowledge, your Bible will be your main source. Devotional guides, teaching, and preaching of the Word are important avenues of spiritual growth. An hour sermon by the Pastor can take hours of study time from devotional material, commentaries, and other study books. Whatever source you choose to gain knowledge from will be enhanced by you studying and reading.

Some people read for development and growth. As much technology as we have in the world today, sometimes it's great to get lost in a good book.

As we read and study to know God, our ability to honor Him will increase in every area of our lives. Reading will help our personal growth in areas of weakness, strength, and responsibility. For example, if we know we are not as versed in an area like health and fitness, all it takes is time to research and gather the information. Then we can apply that information we have gathered.

This is where you have to push yourself to grow beyond the basic principles and move towards advancement.

Whatever your responsibilities are, find books that will allow you to go from being a novice to an expert. The Lord shapes and causes us to grow in many different ways. Still, books are a very significant means of the Lord's grace to us. Everyone has a calling to lead in some area of life, whether that is leadership in the home, church, community, school, workplace or somewhere else. Good leaders are good readers.

The best Christian leaders learn truth, apply that truth, and lead accordingly. The unavoidable fact is your convictions determine how you lead. You will not lead opposite to your convictions. Therefore, we all should continually define, refine and develop our convictions.

Reading is a pleasure worth learning to love and pursue, even if it requires some effort at first. However, whether it is pleasure or pain, commit yourself to read to know, read to grow, read to lead and read to love.

Life Changers

Inspirational Songs:

Call On Jesus ~ Bruce Parham

This Place ~ Tamela Mann

Jesus ~ Le'Andria Johnson

There are people we meet and our personalities connect. We may have just met them but it seems like we have known them all of our lives. Some of these people are life changers. They have personalities that we may want to model and others have character traits we do not want to display. It can be a challenge to deal with all of these personalities day in and day out. It is left up to us to decide how we will act and react when we go throughout our hectic day. Romans 12:18 says, *If it be possible, as much as lieth in you, live peaceably with all men.*

We all have different personality's likes and dislikes. Satan doesn't want any of us to work in unity so you have to be prayed up, and determined that you will not allow people who have the wrong spirit to steal your joy and peace.

These are some personalities or character traits I have encountered that has helped me become a stronger witness for the Lord. I have tried to learn lessons from all of them. You may be able to relate to some of them. Remember you will never have a testimony if you never go through a test.

Praying One - Everyone needs people in their lives that can pray and help them with spiritual guidance. We encounter so many hurting people and so many uncontrollable conditions every day. There is comfort in knowing God will see you through all of the storms of life. Knowing your church family and friends are praying for you will relieve some of your burdens. Prayer is essential for believers and this is one of the joys of being saved. Just to know that God is with you and He is in control of your destiny will bring you peace in every circumstance.

Dedicated Friend - It is truly a blessing to have a friend you can be up front with. They know when something is wrong, even if you don't say it. They can tell it in your voice. This is the person that God has given you to help you through the good and bad days. You can be transparent with this person. They will tell you the good, bad and the ugly. You can count on them to always be honest with you. Whatever they need to do whether it is to pray, speak words of wisdom or encouragement, they have your back. They will not let you down. No matter what you are going through, they are your true friends through thick and thin.

Happy One - This individual is the one that wears a smile ninety-nine percent of the time. They always have a joke to tell you. If they tell you the same joke over and over, you still laugh as if it was the first time hearing it. They are good to be in fellowship with. Their joy seems to overflow and before you know it, you feel better also. Their happiness is contagious!

Needful One - This person is the one that comes or calls only when they need something. They contact you because they feel they can use you for their advantage. They have a tendency to beat around the bush instead of coming right out and asking for what they want. Trust me, they want something or they would not have called.

Event Crasher - This person is usually quiet and sneaky. If you really don't pay attention you might forget they are there. This is the one that will invite themselves to every function whether they are invited or not. Even if it is a R.S.V.P. only event, they are coming. Sometimes they will help and sometimes they won't. But one thing is for sure, they want to be seen. They will say they coordinated the event and did all the work. But really they just came to see what was going on and to network. It really has nothing to do with assisting you. It's all about them.

Boss Hog - This person always wants to be in charge. No one put them in charge but they always seem to be in charge of everything anyway. They are not the boss on your job, at your church, meeting, family function or community event. But if you didn't know it, you would think they are the supervisor, CEO or person you have to report to.

They love to tell others what to do but don't want to do anything. They are truly self-promoted.

Late One - This individual really doesn't value time. When they get there they think they are always on time. Whether they are fifteen minutes or an hour late, it doesn't matter to them. They think that everything is going to start late so they chance it. They have no intentions of ever being on time. This is the person who always wants to help out but you know they are going to be late. If you want them to do something it better be at least an hour after the event starts.

Solo One - This person cannot work with anyone. No matter what group you put them in, they don't seem to get along. They have a problem getting along with others as well as getting along with themselves. If they start out working with someone just give it a little time, they will find a way to end up by themselves. They are always a group of one.

Twenty – Four Hundred/Self Righteous - Instead of having 20/20 vision to see all situations clearly, this person has 20/400 vision. They seem blind to their mistakes but can see everyone else's faults. If you hold a conversation with them, they talk like they really have it all together. If you look closely at what they are involved in, you will notice they are doing what they are condemning others for. Be careful to not open the closet door, all their skeletons will fall out.

Continual Complainer - This individual will complain about any and everything. If you say, "It's a good day", they'll say, "What's good about it?" They have an ungrateful attitude. No matter what you say or try to do to make the situation better nothing is good enough. They seem to magnify the smallest issue and turn it into a major obstacle. Nobody wants to be around this kind of person for too long. This person will steal your joy if you let them. It is very easy to complain about something every day. We all have challenges but things could be a lot worse than they are.

One Up On You - This individual is a person that's alright with you as long as you are on the same level. If you get anything they feel is better than what they have, they get jealous. They will not be happy until they get something of equal value or better than you attained. It's a competition to them. They measure their success by what you have. This is a jealous person. They always want to know about what's new and what's going on with you so that can have an advantage or one up on you.

Nice-Nasty - This person's character depends on what personality trait they decide to show you first. If they are feeling joyful and jubilant, you may encounter the joyful side. If they are having a challenging and complex day, you may see the crabby side. You were unaware of this alter ego but when they show you both sides, believe them.

They usually don't like to apologize. Instead they try to appease you so you can stay friends with them. They are fake and phony. What you see is what you get. You can only keep up the charade for so long. The real you will come out!

Can't Get It Right - This individual gets information incorrect ninety-nine point nine percent of the time. You can tell them a story and it will not be told accurately. You can give them dates, details, and developments and the names, people, and events, will be mixed up, misquoted, and messed up. If you ask them to pick up something for you, it will be the wrong thing from the wrong place, the wrong color, and the wrong size. No matter how many times you tell them when, where and how, they will get it turned, trampled, and transformed into something completely different.

Run and Tell That - This individual can't hold water. They will say, "You can tell me.

I promise I won't tell." Guess what? You already know. They told it. They talk so much they tell what you said, what the other person said and keep talking so much they tell on themselves. When they tell you something it's usually inflated and incorrect. When you hear it again they try and act innocent as if they were not the source of where the information came from. If you told it and they were the only one you disclosed the information to, they are guilty as charged.

Lying/Thief - A liar refuses to tell the truth. They will lie to you right in your face and try to convince you they are telling the truth. Liars tell so many lies they forget what they said and what lie they told. Most liars are charismatic. You can't let your guard down because if you do they will take advantage of it. A thief on the other hand cannot be trusted. They think people don't know what they have or where they left their belongings. They think they have a full proof plan to get what's yours. They will steal things that someone may give them if they would just ask. I remember being a child and the older people would say, "If you will lie, you will steal and if you steal, you will lie."

Two to Ten - This individual has an explosive temper. They are usually nice until you get on a subject where you don't agree with them. Their attitude goes from two to ten in a matter of a few seconds. They have a hard time agreeing to just agree. That's usually not going to happen. If you push that button, when you really don't know you are pushing it, it's over. Their temper explodes and they are very unreasonable. They stay angry for long periods of time. Sometimes they will hold a grudge for years. They don't stay in relationships for long. They seem to have become comfortable being by themselves.

I had to take something back to a store. I needed to exchange some ribbons for a different color. The cashier was speaking rude as well as getting smart with me. I gave her my receipt and she asked me to give her some more money. I inquired as to why she needed me to give her money when it should have been an even exchange. She started yelling and telling me I should have told her my items were on sale. Now mind you, she had the receipt in her hand. So she reluctantly rang up my merchandise again and instead of giving me my bag, she threw my bag and money at me. It took everything I had not to go off. I replied, "I know you didn't just throw my bag and money at me." She kept talking smart and I asked to speak to the manager. She continued talking smart until the manager came up. After I explained to the manager what happened she said she would have the store manager to call me the next day.

I had just watched the movie "Identity Thief" that weekend and satan said, *"Just hit her in the throat."* I was telling myself to stay calm. But once again satan said, *"Just do it. Hit her in the throat and knock her out."* I was so angry. Thank God for keeping me calm through the ordeal. It really could have turned out bad if we started fighting in that store. But praise God I didn't hit her. I had to continue to pray and calm down while I went to my vehicle. It takes fasting and prayer to deal with some people. God is a keeper. We don't have time to lose any battles. God will keep you if you want to be kept.

Words Have Power

Inspirational Songs:

Life And Favor (You Don't Know My Story) John P. Kee and New Life

I Speak Life ~ Donald Lawrence & Company

Encourage Yourself ~ Donald Lawrence & The Tri-City Singers

We speak countless words every day, and pay little attention to what we are really saying. Matthew 12:34 says, *"Out of the abundance of the heart the mouth speaks."* It is important to realize that we are establishing our world by the words we speak. Proverbs 18:21 states, *"Death and life are in the power of the tongue."* If you are wondering why things are not going well for you, you may need to consider what you are speaking.

I tend to look at things from a positive perspective. This particular day I had a meeting with an individual and immediately they began to complain about how bad their day was going. As I sat there listening, they began to look at me and wait for a response. All I could say was "Thank God you made it through all of that, and now it's going to be better."

The person responded, "That's right, you always look at things on the positive side don't you?"

I replied, "Isn't that the best way to look at things? Because things really could be worse."

When difficult situations come up, I try to speak to myself and say, "Lord help me to see whatever circumstances that comes up, it's working for my good." (See Romans 8:28)

My parents taught me to practice saying this scripture when I was young. Now it has become a part of my daily confession. Most people who are around me, know I say regularly, "It's all good." I believe whatever God allows to happen in my life may not always look good or feel good but in the end it is working out for my good. I know God is always working every situation out for me. When tests and trials seem unbearable and I don't feel like saying this I try not to say anything negative. I know any negative words will make matters worse.

During these stressful times you have assurance in knowing that God is going to work everything out. This is the perfect time to say a prayer. I know if God doesn't change the situation, the situation won't change. He will never fail you.

We also need to be watchful of the words we speak to our family, friends, and favorites. Our words can heal or hurt. They can motivate or discourage. Sometimes people speak kinder to coworkers, complete strangers, and friends, but speak harsh to their own family members.

As wives, it is important to speak positive words to our husband when he leaves. He will reflect on those words throughout the day. Our words have a direct effect on the decisions our husbands make.

Negative words linger in peoples' minds for years. If you take the time to reminisce, you will probably remember something someone told you when you were a child. This shows you how much influence words have. The old saying, "sticks and stones may break my bones but words will never hurt me", doesn't seem to be true.

We should make it a daily practice to only allow positive words to come from our mouth. I encourage you today to watch your words more closely. When the devil attacks your mind, let the Word of God flow from your mouth. Don't ever face the attacks of the devil with a closed mouth. Use your words to combat every pitfall and adverse circumstance that the enemy brings to you. That's why it is so important to pray, meditate and know God's Word so we will be able to combat the enemy's attacks.

The enemy will always try to deter you from accomplishing the will of God for your life. He may have already caused you to lose your focus and steal your joy. You may have even allowed thoughts of giving up and thinking life is not worth living anymore to enter your mind. With God living on the inside of you, your heart will be changed and you can make a total transformation of your words, thoughts, and your destiny.

The Pastor's Wife

Inspirational Songs:

I Believe ~ Marvin Sapp

Glorify Him ~ Darwin Hobbs

Sunday Morning Medley ~ Pastor Smokie Norful

I grew up in a Pastor's home and have been married to a pastor for 26 years. Being a (P.K.) Pastor's Kid, I've been in and around the church all of my life. The legacy of Pastor's and ministers is strong in my family. I have brothers, uncles, and cousins who are in ministry. My grandfather was a Senior Pastor and Founder for forty-seven years. My father was Pastor and Founder of his church for twenty-five years. God has a strong presence in the life of my family and I.

Being a Pastor's wife is one of the most challenging endeavors any woman can face. At times it can be difficult finding support and encouragement for the struggles you encounter. I've experienced triumphs, tests, celebrations, tears, accomplishments, trials, struggles, heartaches, and joys of being a wife of a Pastor. God has blessed me to overcome and endure the joys and sorrows of being a Pastor's wife. I want to encourage every Pastor's wife as we continue to walk in our calling that we are unique and God has equipped us for this journey. Buckle up and enjoy the ride!

The Pastor's wife can be the most admired women in the church, and at times the loneliest person in the church. You have to be confident in knowing that you are doing what God called you to do. You will not be everyone's friend. Be mindful that we are all on different spiritual levels. There are some babes in Christ, some growing and learning at different paces, and others may be mature Christians. Thank God for His grace and mercy.

As we attend church and try to work in harmony, it is our responsibility not to let Satan dwell in us. He is coming to church. No one will own up to him coming with them but he will always be there. He is very dedicated to his tri- fold mission to kill, steal and destroy. Just like an invitation only event, Satan will not follow protocol. He will show up before the event starts.

I've seen the good, bad, and the ugly in people who claim to be Christians. I've also seen God do miraculous work in the lives of others. God is real and He is powerful. God can do the impossible in our lives if we allow Him. We all know that when you are following the leading of the Lord, you may not know every step before you take it, but if you have faith, you will end up right where God wants you. The destination will be at the center of His will. Proverbs3:5-6 lets us know if you trust God with all your hearts, He will direct your paths.

When God is working to mold and make you His own there is a process you must be willing to go through. The first step is developing a relationship with God. This requires you to spend time in His Word, seek Him, spend time in prayer and allow Him to totally transform your life. It is a necessity to be born again and repent. This means you must ask God to forgive you of your sins and change your ways. As you are seeking God's will, obedience is key. As a believer God will began to reveal Himself to you. Next, find a Bible based church so you can grow, be taught, mentored and you can find out what your spiritual gifts are. Make sure you stay connected with Christians that you can be in fellowship with. This will allow you to have people you can go to for prayer and support.

Everyone who has a home usually has rules and guidelines in their home. When people don't abide by the rules and guidelines in their home consequences generally follow. Just like in the House of God there are rules and guidelines. God is a God of order. He expects us to read, study, meditate and be obedient to His will. Remember, it's not about us. It's about Jesus. Church should be a place where God is praised, glorified, magnified, and worshipped. God's love should be experienced by all that come through the doors. Lives should be changed, people should be healed and set free, chains should be broken, bad habits banished, miracles experienced, the sick healed, and people should leave the services experiencing God's almighty power so that they can go and be disciples for Christ.

Some of us have turned church into a place where we criticize, judge, manipulate, gossip and act like we shed our own blood for it. I've seen people who think because they give the most money, have the most education, related to the founder of the church, have several gifts, are the longest standing member, be put in charge of a ministry and act like they own the building. Others in leadership act like it's our way or the highway. God forbid. The devil is a liar. I am amazed, speechless at times, ashamed, and disappointed at what I've experienced, seen, and have been told by church members.

I've heard of church fights. I have seen people treat others so bad they said they will never set foot in another church again. I've also seen and heard about people lying and stealing. They disrespect the Pastor and other church leaders in authority.

Some cursing, asking for their tithes and offerings back and getting mad if the church doesn't loan them money, or pay their bills. Some people leave because they couldn't run an auxiliary or ministry the way they wanted. Others act mean, belligerent, spreading all types of rumors while other people try to split the church. The list goes on of the things that have been done in and around church, and people have the nerve to put the name of Jesus in it while they are doing these ungodly things.

It's a shame that you hear people talk about those of us that attend church regularly, say we have been sanctified, and filled with the love of God to act worse than the people who don't know or who has never experienced Jesus in their life. I know that we all are a work in progress but some of the things that are going on in the body of Christ shouldn't be going on. Some people will cause so much division in the church until they split the church. Others will go just to try to stop the progress of the church.

God is not pleased by the disrespectful, unholy, and ungodly behavior that has crept into the church. God is watching and He is not pleased with the behavior of some of us. I would admonish all of us to check ourselves and ask ourselves a question. Am I being a help or a hindrance to my church?

Its time out for (C. M.E.) Christmas, Mother's Day, and Easter Christians. Some of us think we are doing God a favor by attending church. He doesn't need us. God has the power to make rocks praise Him. If we don't praise Him... the stones will cry out! (See Luke 19:40). If you don't have a job in your local church, there is something that can be done to help the progress of your church. It's too many people sitting in the church pews watching a few people do all the work. If you can't line up with the vision that God has given the Pastor of your church, it might be best if you find a church where you can be of better assistance.

God wants to bless us and He can't until we get a willing, obedient spirit and allow Him to create in us a clean heart, and a renewed mind. Jesus is soon to come back. It's praying time. While we are arguing about what color the walls should be painted in the fellowship hall and what color the flowers should be in the foyer, Satan is planning his next attack. If we get off Gossiping Avenue, Complaining Boulevard, Doubting Court, and Self Righteous Street and go to Forgiving Lane, Unity Road, and Deliverance Drive, God will lead us to the Golden Streets of the Pearly Gates to our Heavenly Home.

All it takes is everyone working together on one accord to follow the plans God has for His church. Get your eyes off the problems and put your faith in the Provider. God is able to turn every test into a testimony, every victim into a victorious believer, and any trial into triumph. We can do better if we want. Make up your mind to follow Christ and not the ways of the world.

Being a Pastor's wife is a great joy, responsibility, blessing and high calling. This position comes with great demands. Everyone cannot balance church, home, work, ministry, children, and other goals well. Do what you can to be supportive to your husband, family and the church. God will not put more on you than you can bear (see 1 Corinthians 10:13). He is always there and He will bring you through it all.

I am thankful for God allowing me to be used in this capacity. I have experienced more good days than bad days. Heaven is my goal and with God as a priority, I know my focus. To all the other Pastor's wives, look at the blessings and the one who is sending the blessings. Let God mold you into the Pastor's wife He has called you to be not what other people think you should be. Walk in your calling and let God be pleased with the service you give.

Technology & Social Media

Inspirational Songs:

Keep Me ~ Patrick Dopson

My Joy ~ Tye Tribbett & John P. Kee

Hold On ~ James Fortune & FIYA featuring Monica Fred Hammond

Social networks can help your business, ministry or life in a variety of ways. Traditional marketing mediums such as television commercials, radio, and printed materials are being used less. However, with social media you can connect with targeted customers, family, friends, church, and group members for free. Your only cost is time and energy. Through LinkedIn, Twitter, and Facebook, and other social sites, you can lower your marketing cost. With the increased popularity of social media it is very easy to communicate messages, advertisement articles, blogs, sermons, and other communication. Now you can connect with audiences around the world with a click of your finger. You can connect with like-minded people and create a platform for positive change.

Just like these social sites can be positive, they can have negative effects and lead to addiction. Some people spend countless hours on these sites and neglect their tasks. Some people would rather email, text, send you a message through social media than to have a face to face conversation with you.

I've been in places and someone was in the same room texting me. After a few texts I just stopped responding to them. Then they came over and asked me why I wasn't responding. I politely said, "Excuse me, I'm conversing with this person. If you can be kind enough to give me a few minutes I will talk to you as soon I finish my conversation with this individual. Thank you for being patient with me."

Technology has caused some of us to feel like everything has to come to us in an instant. People seem to want instant gratification. When you look around, you see more and more people looking at that phone instead of paying attention to what they are supposed to be doing. Some of us have experienced people coming in our lane while driving, seen people walk into walls and other people, as well as falling down, and injuring themselves and others.

This is some of the information that has been published about people and their phones.

- People are up about fifteen hours a day, sleep about eight hours and forty-two minutes a day and spend 4.7 hours on their phone.

- Which means on the average, a person spends around one third of their time on their phone.

- The next article stated that twenty-three days a year and 3.9 years of your life is spend looking down at your phone.

- People spend at least 8.4 hours a day on some type of electronic device.

- Some people spend more time in the morning checking emails than eating breakfast

- Nomophobia is the fear of being without a mobile phone or not having a phone signal

- Most cell phones have eighteen times more germs than toilet handles.

- More than forty-five percent of people say they can't live without their phone.

Technology has lowered the motivational level of the people, especially the youth, teenagers, and students. They rely on technology and the internet instead of learning the practical knowledge for everyday life. It's left up to parents to monitor what their children are reading, seeing, and listening to on the internet. People post fights, videos, and other messages that are inappropriate for our children. Another downside of the social media is that some users share too much information which may potentially pose threats to them. Even with all of the tight security settings, your personal information may still be leaked. People can download your pictures and videos and copy them to their status with a few clicks. Sometimes people have so many friends until they may have forgotten that some of their co-workers, supervisors, and members of other affiliations are their friends. People begin to start posting too much information and have gotten terminated from jobs and even gotten in trouble because of something that shouldn't been posted. People should be careful who they accept as friends or followers on social media. It is definitely a wise choice to purge your list of friends from time to time, and change your password also. Some criminals are just waiting on the opportunity to hack your information.

We are in a generation where people love to take selfies. Most of us have experienced people who may ask to use our phone and the next thing you noticed they've started taking selfies. It is still a good practice to ask people do they mind if you take a selfie with their phone and also is it alright if they post a picture or video that they have taken of you on social media before they post it.

If I'm out of town or at an event I usually don't post pictures until after I leave that event. Technology is so advanced now sometimes you don't know someone has taken your picture or even videotaped you. Before you know it you are on Instagram, Twitter, Snapchat, and other social sites. I think almost all of us have experienced this more times than we want to discuss. Asking will keep the doors of communication clear and the confusion to a minimum.

Technology has also helped us in positive ways. There have been times I forgot information I needed for meetings and all I had to do was get the information from my email, phone or tablet. There was a time when it was difficult to get information to someone in another country. Now we don't have to worry, we have so many ways we can connect with others. We can send pictures, videos and urgent messages. Its right at our finger tips. It is easy to reach more people and they can respond back quickly.

It is still good to have backup information like paper directions when you are traveling. Sometimes our phone signal can go out and you are lost without directions to your destination. I've experienced that before. Following your GPS can take you to the wrong place also. Another example is when your phone crashes and you lose important information and all the phone numbers you never remembered or wrote down. That's a miserable feeling when you want and need to connect with someone and you don't have their phone number. So we cannot put all our trust in technology, but it is sure helpful to have.

Even though there are negative impacts and repercussions with technology and social media, it has been beneficial to society as a whole. The world is a better place with the use of technology and social media. As long as we use these in a positive light, the future looks much brighter, using these advancements.

Some people don't want to make changes and adapt to the growing and innovative world we live in. I know that change can be difficult at times but we don't want to be left out of the loop because we refuse to change.

As long as we live we are changing. Change is all around us daily. If we don't change a change is going to come anyway. Don't find yourself walking on the Oregon Trail because you don't want to jump on the Information Highway! In other words, don't stay stuck in the old way because you don't

want to make a change.

Reminiscing/The Good Old Days

Inspirational Songs:

More Than Anything ~ Lamar Campbell & The Spirit Of Praise

I Love The Lord ~ Whitney Houston

Speechless ~ Anita Wilson

Looking back over my life, I didn't know how blessed I was to be brought up in a two parent home where Godly principles were instilled in my siblings and I. In our home going to church was a priority, not an option. My parents taught us to be respectful, honest, hard workers, have good character, and to be dedicated to our family. These are some of the words of wisdom my parents gave

us:

◊Put God first

◊Always pray and consult God for wisdom before

making decisions

◊ If you have some money don't spend it all and

make sure you save some

◊ Walk around your car and check it out before

you take off

◊ Keep gas in your car

◊ Check your fluid levels in your vehicle

◊ Don't loan money to people if you can't afford

for it not to come back to you

◊ Don't argue with a person if you know you are

right

◊ Be on time

◊ If someone is picking you up be ready before the time they are to arrive and don't have them waiting on you

◊ Buy quality things and take care of them

◊ If someone gives you some money to purchase something remember to give them their receipt and their change

◊ Always be a person of your word

My father taught us to never give people money flipped upside down. He said, "Give people their currency with the heads facing in the same direction in ascending or descending order, this will make it easier when you have to count your money." Some other sayings that were frequently spoken were people major in the minor and minor in the majors. People borrow what they need and buy what they want. I didn't know what these things meant back then but I do now.

Being a product of the 60's and 70's, we lived very differently than society lives today. People in the community were like your extended family. If you did something wrong at school you could be disciplined. You knew that if you got out of line an adult was going to put you back in line. Our parents could look at us and we knew what that look meant. We rode our bicycles. The girls played with our Barbie dolls and the boys played with G.I. Joes. We played jacks, marbles, kick ball, dodge ball, volley ball, baseball, basketball, hide and go/seek, hot potato, and tag. We would see the senior citizens playing horse shoes. If someone was getting repairs done on their house we would get a piece of the left over dry wall and use it for sidewalk chalk to draw lines and numbers for hop scotch, and the lines for four square. We would put the younger neighborhood children in the red radio flyer wagon and take them for a walk. We played on the playground and learned how to roller skate at school. We were involved in Girl Scouts/Boys Scout, Junior Achievement, Boys & Girls Club, and attended the activities at the Y.W.C.A. & Y.M.C. A.

After we got home from school we knew to do our homework and chores before we left our house. We didn't have to be told to watch our younger siblings when we were out. That was a given. Everyone knew if an adult said you did something that was law. You couldn't say you didn't do what they said you did. Everyone looked out for each. When we were allowed to play outside, we knew we had to be back home before the street lights came on. It was common practice to see clothes hanging on the line. The neighborhood houses had trees. We would try to climb and get fresh fruit like apples, peaches, cherries or pears. We had a grapevine that grew on the metal fence on the right side of our garage. We couldn't wait to get those big dark purple, sweet, juicy grapes. Most of our parents had gardens with tomatoes, corn, greens, onions, cabbage and cucumbers. Mothers used to cook from scratch. We had homemade biscuits, rolls, pies and pound cake. It was rare to see abandon homes in our community back then. Our community was a village and everyone knew everyone.

Once a friend and I was walking home from junior high school on a hot and muggy, summer day. I had to pass Mr. Cavette's house on the way home. Mr. Cavette (who ended up being my father-in-law) told me after I get home and put my books up to come back and get some corn for my parents. When I got home I got busy and forgot all about what he said he wanted me to do. So the next day when my friend and I were walking home, all of the sudden something came flying pass my face. It startled me. I was ducking so the object would not hit me in the head and jumping up and down at the same time. I saw it was an ear of corn.

Mr. Cavette said "I thought I told you to come back after you put your books up and get this corn for your parents."

I stated, Yes, Sir. You did tell me to come back and I forgot about it." I will be right back."

My friend started laughing all the way home. She said, "I bet you won't forget to go back and get that corn today."

I looked at her and said. "I don't know what's going on with Mr. Cavette, I can't believe he threw that ear of corn at me."

I couldn't wait to get home to tell my mother what just happened. As I picked up my pace I started walking faster. I was just about out of breath when I got to my house. I got to the silver screen door and went up the eight steps, grabbed the door knob and opened the gray wooden door. I put my books down, and started talking so fast my mother couldn't understand a word that I was saying.

She said, "Slow down, catch your breath and tell me what you are saying."

The first thing I said was, "It is something wrong with Mr. Cavette. I think that man is crazy!"

She said, "Why are you calling him crazy."

I replied, "Well! He might not be crazy but I know something is wrong with him. He just threw an ear of corn at me when my friend and I passed by his house a few minutes ago!"

She said, "I'm sure he didn't just throw corn at you for no reason."

I began to tell her about the conversation we had on the previous day. I mentioned that he told me to come back to pick up some corn for her and Dad. I told her I got busy and forgot to go back and get it. She asked if I was alright. I told her I was fine after I jumped and dodged the flying corn.

She replied, "I'm sure he didn't mean any harm." She laughed and said, "I think you need to get a brown paper bag out of the cabinet and go down the street and get that corn from Mr. Cavette."

In those days parents used to share the food they had with the other neighbors. We used the bartering system. What happened to everyone looking out for each other?

There was always an inquisitive neighbor who knew the comings and goings of everyone. It was usually the neighbor that was home all the time. I call those neighbors The Kravitz's. They didn't miss anything that happened in the neighborhood. Just like on the old television sitcom *Bewitched*, if Mrs. Gladys Kravitz saw something, she would immediately call her husband to come and see what was going on at Samantha and Darrin Stephen's house. As children we thought they were just being nosey neighbors but they were as good as a Neighborhood Task Force. That is one key element that is missing today, care and concern for others.

As I take notice of how we treat one another in the 21st Century. I wondered when things changed. Where did the breakdown of the family take place? It is left up to us to instruct our children and give them the correct guidance. We cannot expect anybody else to do it for us.

I see children telling their parents what they will and won't do. That was unheard of in our generation. The schools are having challenges with educating our youth today. They took prayer out of school, and have put the police in the schools. Society wants to tell you how to discipline your children. When I go in the school I see teachers who are excited and passionate about teaching and others who seem to be fed up and just there for a paycheck. Studies have shown society is writing our children off as failures as early as the third grade. We cannot afford to sit back and allow this behavior to continue. It's time to take our family and children back.

This is the old school teachings verses the new school teachings. This may take your mind back to the good old days. Take a trip down memory lane.

OLD SCHOOL	NEW SCHOOL
What goes on in our house, stays in our house.	Children tell everything they hear and see.
Say hello before you ask to speak to the person you are calling.	Without saying hello first, they ask for the person they want to speak with.
We were not allowed to go in other people's homes if a parent or adult was not there.	Children come over and come in all times of the day and night.
Walk around your vehicle.	People just get in the vehicle and take off. They don't check or look at all.
Brush your teeth. Clean your ears. Put on clean underwear. Keep your body clean.	Some children don't take baths or shower regularly.
Always clean up after yourself.	Leave everything a mess.
Close all doors you open.	Leave doors open (to the house, car, cabinets, etc.).
Knock on a door before entering (especially closed doors).	Come in without knocking, just barge in.

When grown-ups are talking, you were not allowed in their conversation or in the same room.	Children are in your face while grown-ups are talking, answering questions you ask the parent/adult.
Don't ask for something you don't see on the table.	Now children ask for everything ketchup, hot sauce, etc. example: I don't eat _____ without_____!
When you get paid, put your tithes aside 1st, then fill up your vehicle or pay bills.	Now people put in enough gas in their vehicle to get to their destination. People rarely fill their car up.
Always tell the truth no matter what you did.	Lie and hope the truth never comes out.
We were taught 15 minutes is a quarter until or a quarter after the hour (time).	Young people think a quarter is 25 minutes to the hour or 25 minutes after the hour.
We taught washing the dishes meant wash all the dishes in the house, clean all counters, wipe down the stove and refrigerator, and sweep/mop the floor.	Now all they do is wash the dishes. They don't check for any other dishes anywhere else in the house.

We were taught how to properly do laundry. You had to separate them by colors and wash the bedding separate. We also knew what temperature to wash and dry clothing on and what detergent/bleach went on which clothing.	Now they wash everything together and don't change the temperature at all. Everything gets dried on high.
Men's shoes were clean and polished.	Now children walk on the back of their shoes. They don't tie their laces. Some children will trip over the laces before they will tie them.
Push you chair in after you get up from the table.	Now chairs are left out.
We were taught to sit down (right) in a chair.	Now children sit on their knees or stand up.
We were taught to pray (say grace) before we ate.	No prayer, just start eating.
Pray before we go to bed.	No prayer, just go to sleep.

We were taught keep your hands to yourself and don't touch anything when you go in a store.	Now children pick up items, holler, scream, and fall out if you don't buy it.
Don't go out the house with rollers or curlers in your hair, scarves (or bonnets) on your head.	Now you see people in public looking any kind of way.
Pajamas were worn for sleeping not outside wear. Beaters (men) were underwear.	People wear pajamas like they are regular pants, and beaters are worn like regular shirts.
We were taught to eat all our food before we could get something to drink.	Now children will become full from drinking before they eat their meal.
We had to eat what was cooked, no choice of a different food.	Now each child will ask for something different; everyone eating a different entrée.
We were taught after you ate dinner, you cleaned up and didn't go back into the kitchen dirtying up dishes. No dirty dishes were left in	Now children don't care. They will leave every dish dirty if you let them.

the sink. The kitchen was clean before bed.	
If our parents found too many dirty dishes after you washed them, they would take all of the dishes out of the cabinet and make you wash them again.	Children act like they didn't wash the dishes if you find them in the cabinet dirty.
If you turn a light on, turn it off.	No lights are turned off they are left on all day.
We were taught to respect all adults.	They feel you have to earn respect to get respect.
We were disciplined (spanked, chastised, or whooped).	Now children only get a timeout.
We were taught our timetables before we left the third grade.	Some teenagers still do not know them.
We were taught to say, "Yes Ma'am", "No Ma'am", "Yes Sir and No Sir".	Now children respond, "What, yes, no." Or they ignore you and just look as if you're not talking to them.
We all ate at the dinner table as a family.	Now children eat all over the house,

	bedroom, family room, den, etc.
We were taught to make up your bed when you get up and out of it in the morning.	Now children may pull the cover up on the bed (on a good day), it is not usually made up every day.
We were taught to walk on the sidewalk and not on people's lawns (grass).	Now people walk in the street not on the sidewalk and they look at you like they wish you would hit them.
We were taught if clothing had a belt loop you need to wear a belt.	Now people wear sagging pants like other people want to see their underwear.
We were taught to eat everything that was put on your plate before you get up from the table.	Now children will tell you what they want /don't want to eat and what portion size they want.

Talking Clay (A Conversation With God)

Inspirational Songs:

Saved ~ Deitrick Haddon

Lord Do It ~ John P. Kee and the New Life Community Choir

Yes ~ Shekinah Glory

God is the potter and we are the clay (see Isaiah 64:8). We are fearfully and wonderfully made (see Psalms 139:14). Just like a potter takes a piece of clay and rolls, stretches, flips and turns it, that is what the Lord wants to do in our lives. He wants to transform us into a vessel to use for His glory. We pray and ask God for direction and He gives us specific instructions.

When God says, "Turn right," we turn left.

He says, "Stop," we keep going.

He says, "Turn around. I'm redirecting you to your purpose," we head straight to a head on collision, which could have been avoided if we had of took heed to what He was saying.

At times it may seem as if God is not listening to or answering our prayers. But He is! When you decide to get closer to God, the farther you will get from people and the distractions that are holding you back.

Every time you take matters in your own hands you are telling God, "I can handle this. You don't have to worry about this situation. I've got this."

He's such a gentlemen. He will not go against your will. He will let you do what you want. When we take control of our lives we end up lonely, broken, confused, and hurt. All we have to do is be obedient. It sounds simple but it is very hard for some of us to do. If we look back in retrospect at some of the things we got involved in, God was warning us before those things happened. That relationship that left you broken, that person that was never faithful, the decision you made after being advised against it, the job you took because they were the first company that contacted you, and signing contracts without being informed of the consequences - all these situations are lessons. Some of us learn the hard way. Some of us learn the first time and others seem like we will never learn.

At times we act just like Jonah and disobey God. He knew God wanted him to go to Nineveh but he went down to Joppa, found a ship going to Tarshish, paid the fare, to go with them to Tarshish from the presence of the LORD (see Jonah1:1-3). We know what we are supposed to be doing but have a tendency to do the opposite of what God instructs us to do. We make all kinds of excuses why we can't do what He has told us to do. God has given each of us enough love to love the unlovable. We are the right height to climb over every obstacle that we encounter. He has given all of us dreams and aspirations that we can achieve by His grace. Our feet are the correct proportioned to walk into our destiny. So we need to stop allowing the enemy to make us feel inferior.

The challenges of life will cause us to have a personal conversation with God.

This is the conversation of the Talking Clay and the Potter:

The Clay: "Lord I asked you for children to nurture, guide, and give direction."

Potter: "I gave you them and you were too busy to raise and give them correction."

The Clay: "Lord, I need You to lead and be my guide."

Potter: "I sent my Spirit, but His presence you pushed aside."

The Clay: "I asked You for a spouse to have and to hold."

Potter: "You didn't give any affection and allowed My love to grow cold."

The Clay: "I prayed for another job. Lord, I could use some extra money."

Potter: "I gave you a new promotion and now you are acting funny."

Clay: "Lord, I need someone to talk to, can you give me a friend?"

Potter: "I've always been there and I'll be with you to the very end!"

We ask God for countless things but if He doesn't give us what we want when we want it, we shut Him out, cry, complain, get angry, and even leave. All God wants is a yes, not a no, maybe, or later. When you say yes to God, everything else will fall into place. If you are wondering what is taking so long, God is just waiting on you. He's been ready to bless you. All you have to do is stop taking control of everything. Let God turn what was just a dull and dingy lump of clay into a designer's masterpiece. God will mend every broken piece in your life. Will you surrender your will and say, "Yes?"

Satisfied With The Wrong Man

God made you a woman to give life and birth and possibilities.

Lady's stop being:

Sunday's Substitute

Monday's Moment

Tuesday's Temptation

Wednesday's Wish

Thursday's Tease

Friday's Fling

Saturday's Sometimes

Let God bless you with a husband to be:

Sunday's Soulmate

Monday's Memories

Tuesday's Thoughts

Wednesday's Woman

Thursday's Treasure

Friday's Forever

Saturday's Significance

You will never be the Woman God intended for you to be, if you keep allowing yourself to be with the wrong man. Don't settle for Mr. Part-time Pleasure when you really want Mr. Full-time Fulfillment.

Satisfaction Survey

4=Strongly Agree   3=Agree   2=Disagree   1=Neutral

	4	3	2	1
I am satisfied with the way things are going in my life right now				
I am satisfied with my relationship with my family				
I am satisfied with my physical health				
I am satisfied with my spiritual health				
I am satisfied with my mental health				
I know what my purpose is in life				
I know what my gifts and talents are				
I find ways to develop my gifts and talents				
I am a trustworthy person				
I have a mentor/mentee				
I believe in God				
I use my gifts and talents to help others				
I attend church regularly				
I have a good support system				
I am an optimistic person				
I am an pessimistic person				

I am a good communicator				
If something is bothering me I usually keep things to myself				
I am able to quickly forgive and move on				
I try something new every four months				
I reward myself if I do something good				
I incorporate laughter into my day				
I go on vacations or outings regularly				
I let my family and friends know I love and appreciate them				
I compliment other people regularly				
I am happy in the relationship that I am presently in				
I read a book, newspaper, magazine or study regularly				
I exercise regularly				
I am up to date with my physicals, doctor, and dental visits				
I have a journal and write regularly				
I am an organized person				

After you add up your score, look back at the things you scored the highest and lowest on. Ask yourself are you satisfied/dissatisfied and make the necessary changes. With God you can live a life of satisfaction.

Don't go another day being

satisfied with not being satisfied.

Book/Songs

Chapter ~ Title	Song	Artist
Eye Opener	Never A Day	United Tenors
	When You Praise	Fred Hammond
	The Mender	Donald Lawrence
Leaving The Past	Wait On Him	John P. Kee & New Life Comm. Choir
	There Is A King In You	Donald Lawrence
	Full And Complete	Walter Hawkins & The Love Center Choir
Marriage	Lost Without You	BeBe & CeCe Winans
	Wedding Song	John P. Kee & New Life Community Choir
	Just For Me	Karen Clark Sheard
Your Spouse - Your Friend	Constantly	Rev. Clay Evans & The AARC Choir
	Spiritual	Donald Lawrence
	Healing	Kelly Price

Forgiveness	Peace Be Still	Vanessa Bell Armstrong
	Perfect Peace	Keith Pringle
	Total Praise	Richard Smallwood
Know Your Worth	I Can't Forget	Denitra Champ
	Worth	Anthony Brown & Group therAPy
	Thank You	Walter Hawkins & The Love Center Choir
Relationships	Show Me The Way	New Jerusalem Baptist Church Choir
	We'll Understand It Better	Kenneth Martin and The Voices in Praise
	Heaven	Bishop Neal Roberson & The Macedonia Mass Choir
Mentor/ Mentee	Jesus Will	Anita Wilson
	God Is Great	Ricky Dillard and New G
	God's Got A Blessing	Norman Hutchins

Healthy Nuts And Seeds	No Defeat	Hezekiah Walker
	I'm Good	Tim Bowman Jr.
	Overflow	Pastor William Murphy III
Knowing Your Purpose	My Name Is Victory	Jonathan Nelson
	Go Get It	Mary Mary
	Work Out For My Good (Live)	Dorinda Clark-Cole
We Are The Teacher	Bring Back The Days of Yea and Nay	The Winans
	Good and Bad	J. Moss
	Coming Back Home	BeBe Winans *Featuring Brian McKnight and Joe*
Prayer	The Prayer	Donnie McClurkin and Yolanda Adams
	Standing In The Need	John P. Kee and The New Life Community Choir
	Pray	CeCe Winans
Music And The Moment	Everything You Touch Is A Song	The Winans

	Every Praise	Hezekiah Walker
	I Will Bless The Lord	Byron Cage
Your Heart	Create In Me	Lawrence K. Matthews
	When Sunday Comes	Donald Lawrence & The Tri-City Singers *Featuring Darryl Coley*
	Your Will	Darius Brooks
Your Mind	Still Here	The Williams Brothers
	Ain't No Need To Worry	Rueben Studdard
	It's All God	Soul Seekers Featuring Marvin Winans
Reading	Being With You	Marcus Cole
	I Worship Thee	John P. Kee
	Hear My Voice	Rance Allen Group
Life Changers	Call on Jesus	Bruce Parham
	This Place	Tamela Mann
	Jesus	Le'Andria Johnson
Words Have Power	Life And Favor (You Don't Know My Story)	John P. Kee & New Life

	I Speak Life	Donald Lawrence & Company
	Encourage Yourself	Donald Lawrence & The Tri-City Singers
Pastor's Wife	I Believe	Marvin Sapp
	Glorify Him	Darwin Hobbs
	Sunday Morning Medley	Smokie Norful
Technology/Social Media	Keep Me	Patrick Dopson
	My Joy	Tye Tribbett & John P. Kee
	Hold On	James Fortune & FIYA *Featuring Monica &Fred Hammond*
Reminiscing/The Good Old Days	More Than Anything	Lamar Campbell & The Spirit Of Praise
	I Love The Lord	Whitney Houston
	Speechless	Anita Wilson
Talking Clay (A Conversation With God)	Saved	Deitrick Haddon

	Lord Do It	John P. Kee and the New Life Community Choir
	Yes	Shekinah Glory

Author Bio

Sandra has worked in retail management and in the public and charter schools. Working with children for over 40 years, she has taught regular education as well as special education students. She works alongside her husband in ministry as Director of Women's Ministry, Praise Team Director, and in other various capacities.

Sandra attained a Bachelor's Degree from University of Michigan Flint and a Master's Degree in Educational Leadership from Eastern Michigan University. .Her business Personalized Just 4 U, is a tool that God has blessed her with to be a blessing to the Body of Christ. Her Book Club (G.E.M.S.)

Getting Empowered for Ministry and Service is a tool that God has given her to mentor and minister to women from all works of life.

Sandra D. Cavette is an author, mentor, conference speaker and entrepreneur from Flint, Michigan. She has been married to the love of her life Pastor Gregory L. Cavette Sr. for 32 years. She is also the mother of four children.

Bibliography

Book Info about Music

Research information about Music

1) Article ~ Music Is Good For You   Making Music work for you.

*Source: Research was conducted by VisionCritical in April 2012 among 1,000 UK businesses and Entertainment Media Research in 2009 among 2,000 UK consumers. EMR also conducted the research in 2010 among 400 small retailers, hairdressers, offices and factories.

2) Article ~ *Music has become an important competitive tool for business owners.*

Custom Channels World HQ

2569 Park Lane, Suite 104
Lafayette, Colorado 80026 (303) 444-7700
info@CustomChannels.net

~Rules of Common Courtesy by Derek Huether
May 21, 2010

www.ingramcontent.com/pod-product-compliance
Lightning Source LLC
Chambersburg PA
CBHW051825090426
42736CB00011B/1647